To:

From:

Horses
Are Special

GRAMERCY BOOKS
NEW YORK

Published by Gramercy Books, an imprint of Random House Value Publishing, a division of Random House, Inc., New York.

Gramercy is a registered trademark and the colophon is a trademark of Random House, Inc.

Random House
New York • Toronto • London • Sydney • Auckland
www.randomhouse.com

Compiled by Kira Baum
Interior design by Christine Kell

Printed and bound in China

Library of Congress Cataloging-in-Publication Data

Horses are special : a tribute to our noble companions.
    p. cm.
    ISBN: 978-0-517-22884-5
    1. Horses—Quotations, maxims, etc. 2. Horses—Pictorial works.

PN6084.H66H68 2007
636.1—dc22

2006043535

10 9 8 7 6 5 4 3 2 1

Acknowledgments: 1, *Ingram Publishing/Alamy*. 3, *Medioimages/Alamy*. 5, *M Stock/Alamy*. 7, *Masterfile*. 9, *Digital Vision/SuperStock*. 11, *Inc. MAXX IMAGES/SuperStock*. 12-13, *Purestock/SuperStock*. 14, *Juniors Bildarchiv/Alamy*. 17, *Jacque Denzer Parker/Index Stock*. 19, *Lisette Le Bon/SuperStock*. 21, *Pixtal/age fotostock*. 22, *Juniors Bildarchiv/Alamy*. 24-25, *Pixtal/age fotostock*. 27, *Creatas/Jupiter Images*. 29, *Photos.com Select/Index Stock*. 31, *Stockbyte/Punchstock*. 32-33, *Comstock Images/Jupiter Images*. 34, *Juniors Bildarchiv/Alamy*. 37, *Goodshoot/Jupiter Images*. 39, *Masterfile*. 40-41, *Masterfile*. 43, *Pixtal/age fotostock*. 44, *Creatas/Jupiter Images*. 47, *Ingram Publishing/Alamy*. 49, *Pixtal/age fotostock*. 50-51, *Masterfile*. 53, *Corbis/Punchstock*. 55, *Purestock/SuperStock*. 56, *Comstock/SuperStock*. 58-59, *Comstock Images/Jupiter Images*. 61, *Corbis*. 63, *imagebroker/Alamy*. 64, *Ingram Publishing/SuperStock*.

Horses
Are Special

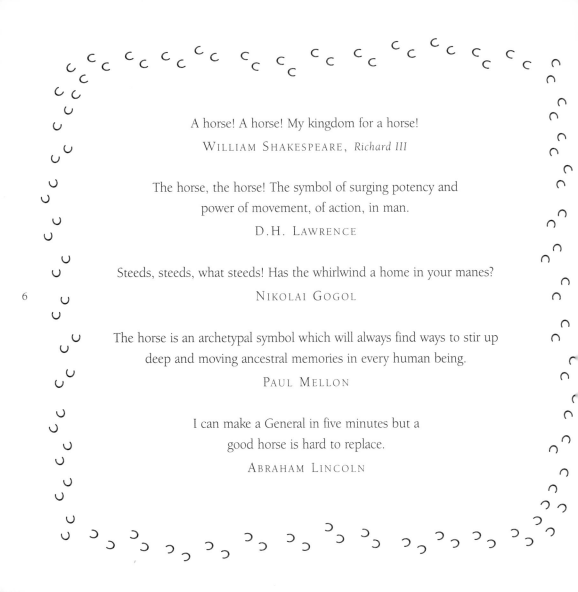

A horse! A horse! My kingdom for a horse!

WILLIAM SHAKESPEARE, *Richard III*

The horse, the horse! The symbol of surging potency and
power of movement, of action, in man.

D.H. LAWRENCE

Steeds, steeds, what steeds! Has the whirlwind a home in your manes?

NIKOLAI GOGOL

6

The horse is an archetypal symbol which will always find ways to stir up
deep and moving ancestral memories in every human being.

PAUL MELLON

I can make a General in five minutes but a
good horse is hard to replace.

ABRAHAM LINCOLN

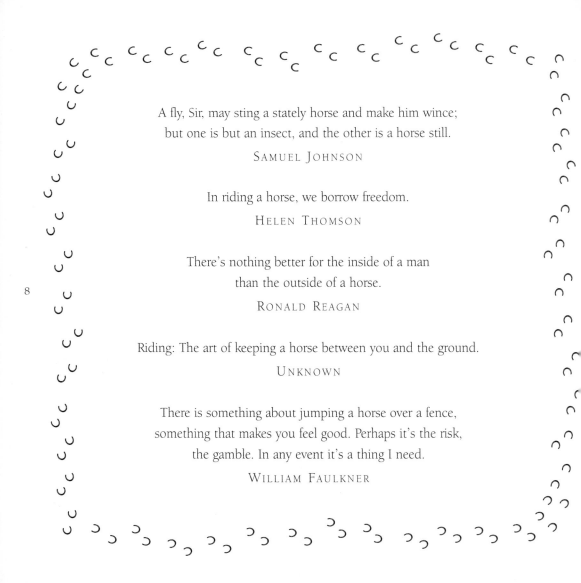

A fly, Sir, may sting a stately horse and make him wince;
but one is but an insect, and the other is a horse still.

SAMUEL JOHNSON

In riding a horse, we borrow freedom.

HELEN THOMSON

There's nothing better for the inside of a man
than the outside of a horse.

RONALD REAGAN

Riding: The art of keeping a horse between you and the ground.

UNKNOWN

There is something about jumping a horse over a fence,
something that makes you feel good. Perhaps it's the risk,
the gamble. In any event it's a thing I need.

WILLIAM FAULKNER

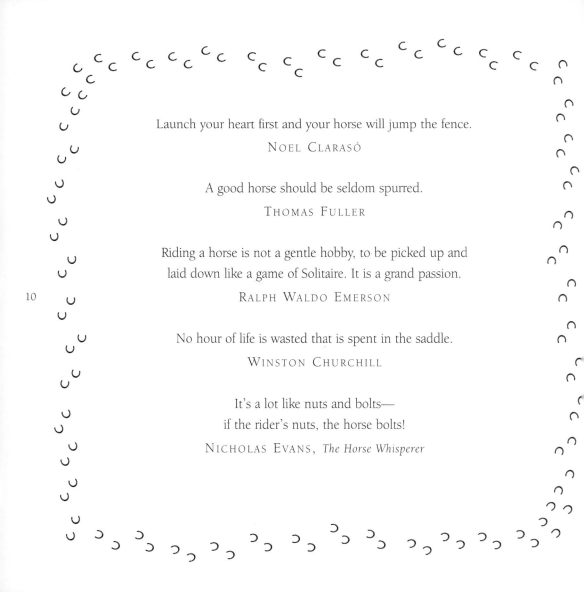

Launch your heart first and your horse will jump the fence.

NOEL CLARASÓ

A good horse should be seldom spurred.

THOMAS FULLER

Riding a horse is not a gentle hobby, to be picked up and
laid down like a game of Solitaire. It is a grand passion.

RALPH WALDO EMERSON

No hour of life is wasted that is spent in the saddle.

WINSTON CHURCHILL

It's a lot like nuts and bolts—
if the rider's nuts, the horse bolts!

NICHOLAS EVANS, *The Horse Whisperer*

Strong Men, riding horses. In the West
On a range five hundred miles. A Thousand. Reaching
From dawn to sunset.

GWENDOLYN BROOKS, "Strong Men, Riding Horses"

A cowboy is a man with guts and a horse.

WILLIAM JAMES

In Westerns you were permitted to kiss your horse but never your girl.

GARY COOPER

There has to be a woman, but not much of a one.
A good horse is much more important.

MAX BRAND, on writing Westerns

Treat a horse like a woman and a woman like a horse.
And they'll both win for you.

ELIZABETH ARDEN

Hurrah! Hurrah for Sheridan!
Hurrah! Hurrah for horse and man!

THOMAS BUCHANAN READ, "Sheridan's Ride"

Travis Coates: Now Papa, you know I've been aching all over for a
                good horse to ride. I've told you time and again.
Jim Coates: What you're needing more than a horse is a good dog.
Travis Coates: Yes sir, but what I'm wanting most is a horse.
Jim Coates: Alright, you act a man's part and I'll bring you a
                man's horse.

Old Yeller

Blind with love, my daughter
has cried nightly for horses,
whose long-necked marchers and churners
that she has mastered, any and all,
reigning them in like a circus hand....

ANNE SEXTON

16

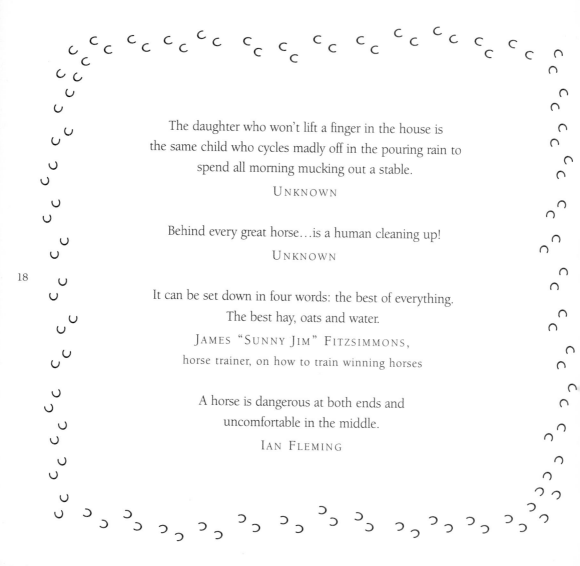

The daughter who won't lift a finger in the house is
the same child who cycles madly off in the pouring rain to
spend all morning mucking out a stable.

UNKNOWN

Behind every great horse…is a human cleaning up!

UNKNOWN

It can be set down in four words: the best of everything.
The best hay, oats and water.

JAMES "SUNNY JIM" FITZSIMMONS,
horse trainer, on how to train winning horses

A horse is dangerous at both ends and
uncomfortable in the middle.

IAN FLEMING

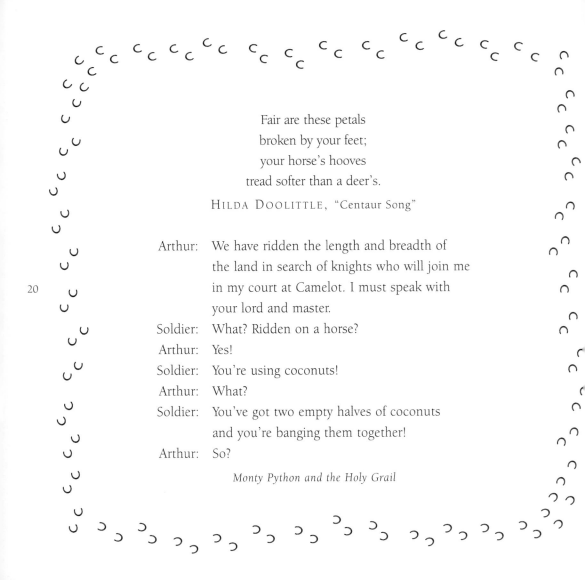

Fair are these petals
broken by your feet;
your horse's hooves
tread softer than a deer's.

HILDA DOOLITTLE, "Centaur Song"

Arthur: We have ridden the length and breadth of
          the land in search of knights who will join me
          in my court at Camelot. I must speak with
          your lord and master.
Soldier: What? Ridden on a horse?
Arthur: Yes!
Soldier: You're using coconuts!
Arthur: What?
Soldier: You've got two empty halves of coconuts
          and you're banging them together!
Arthur: So?

          Monty Python and the Holy Grail

Work's good, builds character. I wouldn't want him drifting through life....A horse has got to learn to stand on his own four feet.

WILBUR POST, *Mister Ed*

She knew that the horse, born to serve nobly,
had waited in vain for someone noble to serve. His spirit
knew that nobility had gone out of men.

D.H. LAWRENCE

When I was a kid, if a guy got killed in a western movie
I always wondered who got his horse.

GEORGE CARLIN

What is a horse shoe? What does a horse shoe do?
Are there any horse socks? Is anybody listening to me?

Billy Madison

If you're a horse, and someone gets on you, and falls off, and then gets right back on you, I think you should buck him off right away.

JACK HANDEY

I voted for *Seabiscuit* [for Best Costume Design]. That's the most realistic horse costume I've ever seen.

BILLY CRYSTAL, The 76th Annual Academy Awards

I realize that the concept of wild horses probably stirs romantic notions in many of you, but this is because you have never met any wild horses in person…They amble up to your camp site, and their attitude is: "We're wild horses. We're going to eat your food, knock down your tent and poop on your shoes. We're protected by federal law, just like Richard Nixon."

DAVE BARRY

You don't have to say your horse told you.
Tell her it was your cat.

MISTER ED

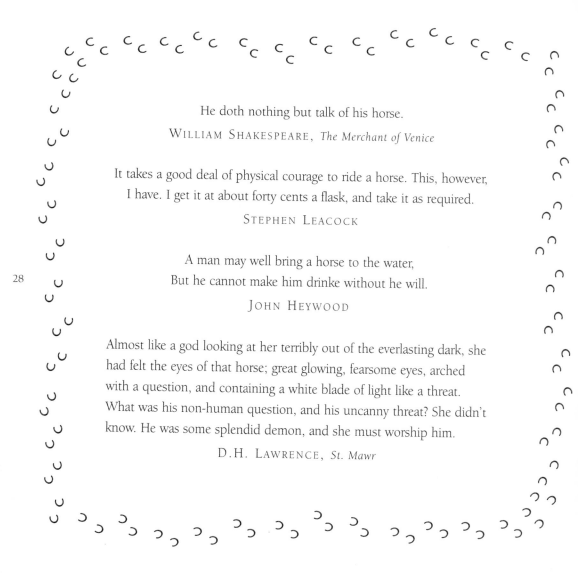

He doth nothing but talk of his horse.

WILLIAM SHAKESPEARE, *The Merchant of Venice*

It takes a good deal of physical courage to ride a horse. This, however,
I have. I get it at about forty cents a flask, and take it as required.

STEPHEN LEACOCK

A man may well bring a horse to the water,
But he cannot make him drinke without he will.

JOHN HEYWOOD

Almost like a god looking at her terribly out of the everlasting dark, she
had felt the eyes of that horse; great glowing, fearsome eyes, arched
with a question, and containing a white blade of light like a threat.
What was his non-human question, and his uncanny threat? She didn't
know. He was some splendid demon, and she must worship him.

D.H. LAWRENCE, *St. Mawr*

I thought that the chief thing to be done in order to
equal boys was to be learned and courageous. So I decided
to study Greek and learn to manage a horse.

ELIZABETH CADY STANTON

The story is told of a man who, seeing one of the thoroughbred
stables for the first time, suddenly removed his hat and said in awed
tones, "My Lord! The cathedral of the horse."

Kentucky: A Guide to the Bluegrass State

What do I believe in? Would it really interest you? Oh, a lot of things.
A good horse. Steak and kidney pudding.

REGINALD DENNY as George Brown in *The Lost Patrol*

You gotta excuse Comet. He still doesn't realize he's a horse.

BRISCO COUNTY JR., *The Adventures of Brisco County Jr.*

A fiery horse with the speed of light, a cloud of dust and a hearty "Hi-yo Silver"—the Lone Ranger!

The Lone Ranger

I got a horse and the west is wide.

Billy the Kid

One nice thing about a horse is that its body won't rust after just one winter on salted roads.

ANONYMOUS

I don't even like old cars…I'd rather have a…horse. A horse is at least human, for God's sake.

J.D. SALINGER, *The Catcher in the Rye*

People on horses look better than they are. People in cars look worse than they are.

UNKNOWN

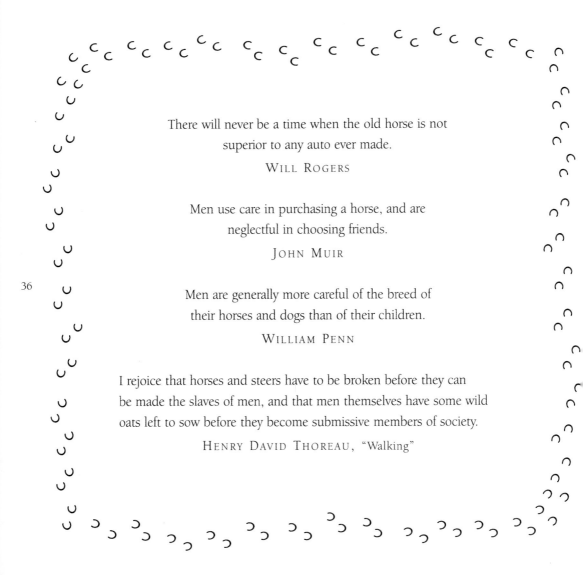

There will never be a time when the old horse is not
superior to any auto ever made.

WILL ROGERS

Men use care in purchasing a horse, and are
neglectful in choosing friends.

JOHN MUIR

Men are generally more careful of the breed of
their horses and dogs than of their children.

WILLIAM PENN

I rejoice that horses and steers have to be broken before they can
be made the slaves of men, and that men themselves have some wild
oats left to sow before they become submissive members of society.

HENRY DAVID THOREAU, "Walking"

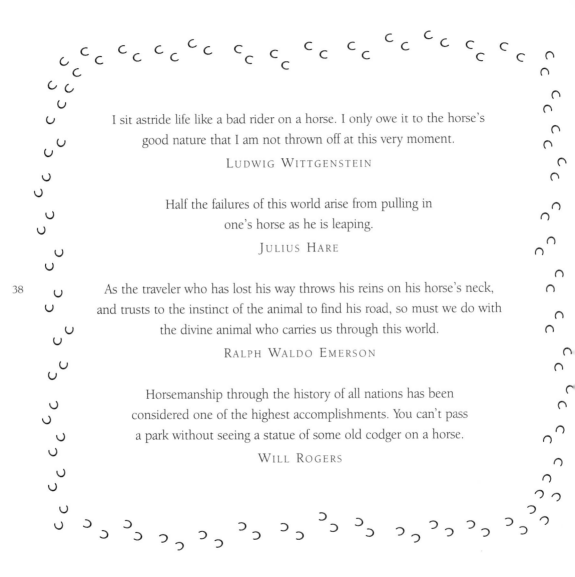

I sit astride life like a bad rider on a horse. I only owe it to the horse's
good nature that I am not thrown off at this very moment.

LUDWIG WITTGENSTEIN

Half the failures of this world arise from pulling in
one's horse as he is leaping.

JULIUS HARE

As the traveler who has lost his way throws his reins on his horse's neck,
and trusts to the instinct of the animal to find his road, so must we do with
the divine animal who carries us through this world.

RALPH WALDO EMERSON

Horsemanship through the history of all nations has been
considered one of the highest accomplishments. You can't pass
a park without seeing a statue of some old codger on a horse.

WILL ROGERS

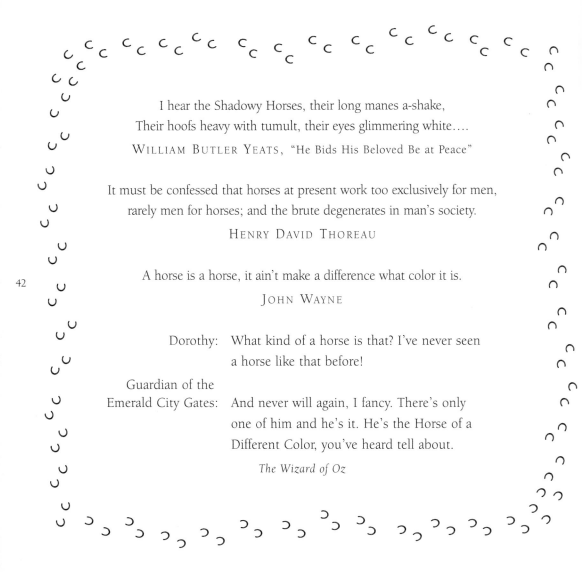

I hear the Shadowy Horses, their long manes a-shake,
Their hoofs heavy with tumult, their eyes glimmering white....

WILLIAM BUTLER YEATS, "He Bids His Beloved Be at Peace"

It must be confessed that horses at present work too exclusively for men,
rarely men for horses; and the brute degenerates in man's society.

HENRY DAVID THOREAU

A horse is a horse, it ain't make a difference what color it is.

JOHN WAYNE

Dorothy: What kind of a horse is that? I've never seen
a horse like that before!

Guardian of the
Emerald City Gates: And never will again, I fancy. There's only
one of him and he's it. He's the Horse of a
Different Color, you've heard tell about.

The Wizard of Oz

Mrs. Finney: Sadie's right. That track's crooked.
Lora May: It isn't the track, it's the horses. They fix
things up amongst themselves.

A Letter To Three Wives

Four things greater than all things are—
Women and Horses and Power and War

RUDYARD KIPLING, "The Ballad of the King's Jest"

I got quite bored, serving in the bar. Since I was there, the
customers wouldn't talk about women, and with half their subject
matter denied them, it was: horses, silence; horses, silence.

BERNADETTE DEVLIN

What do we, as a nation, care about books? How much
do you think we spend altogether on our libraries, public or
private, as compared with what we spend on our horses?

JOHN RUSKIN

45

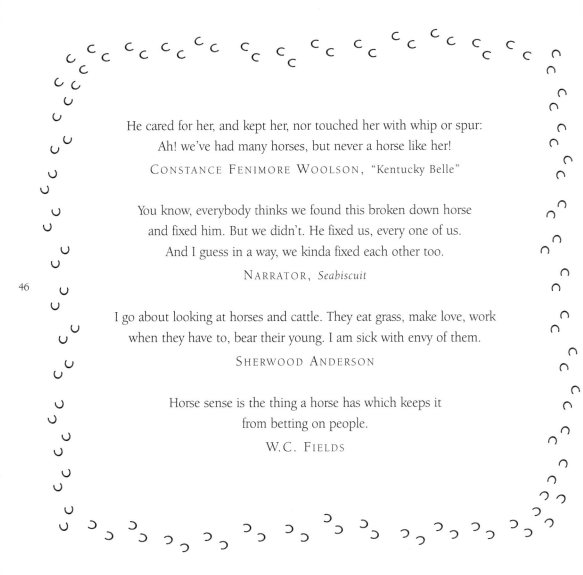

He cared for her, and kept her, nor touched her with whip or spur:
Ah! we've had many horses, but never a horse like her!
CONSTANCE FENIMORE WOOLSON, "Kentucky Belle"

You know, everybody thinks we found this broken down horse
and fixed him. But we didn't. He fixed us, every one of us.
And I guess in a way, we kinda fixed each other too.
NARRATOR, *Seabiscuit*

I go about looking at horses and cattle. They eat grass, make love, work
when they have to, bear their young. I am sick with envy of them.
SHERWOOD ANDERSON

Horse sense is the thing a horse has which keeps it
from betting on people.
W.C. FIELDS

46

Horse sense, n.: Stable thinking.

UNKNOWN

Reckless automobile driving arouses the suspicion that much of the
horse sense of the good old days was possessed by the horse.

UNKNOWN

Horses and children, I often think, have a lot of
the good sense there is in the world.

JOSEPHINE DEMOTT ROBINSON

A horse never runs so fast as when he has
other horses to catch up and outpace.

OVID

To deny, to believe, and to doubt absolutely—
this is for man what running is for a horse.

BLAISE PASCAL

A man that don't love a horse, there is
something the matter with him.

WILL ROGERS

To my way of thinking there's something wrong, or missing, with any
person who hasn't got a soft spot in their heart for an animal of some
kind. With most folks the dog stands highest as man's friend, then comes
the horse, with others the cat is liked best as a pet, or a monkey is fussed
over; but whatever kind of animal it is a person likes, it's all hunky-dory
so long as there's a place in the heart for one or a few of them.

WILL JAMES, *Smoky, the Cow Horse*

The wagon rests in winter, the sleigh in summer, the horse never.

YIDDISH PROVERB

Many people have sighed for the 'good old days' and
regretted the 'passing of the horse,' but today, when only those
who like horses own them, it is a far better time for horses.

C.W. ANDERSON

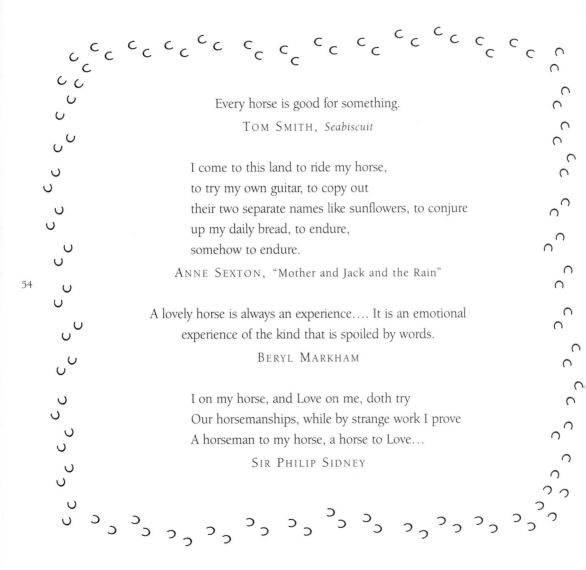

Every horse is good for something.

TOM SMITH, *Seabiscuit*

I come to this land to ride my horse,
to try my own guitar, to copy out
their two separate names like sunflowers, to conjure
up my daily bread, to endure,
somehow to endure.

ANNE SEXTON, "Mother and Jack and the Rain"

A lovely horse is always an experience.... It is an emotional
experience of the kind that is spoiled by words.

BERYL MARKHAM

I on my horse, and Love on me, doth try
Our horsemanships, while by strange work I prove
A horseman to my horse, a horse to Love...

SIR PHILIP SIDNEY

We judge a horse not only by its pace on a racecourse,
but also by its walk, nay, when resting in its stable.

MICHEL DE MONTAIGNE

God forbid that I should go to any heaven in which
there are no horses.

R.B. CUNNINGHAME GRAHAM

If your horse says no, you either asked the wrong question,
or asked the question wrong.

PAT PARELLI

Jack: We'll ride horses on the beach, right in the surf.
Now, but you'll have to do it like a real cowboy.
None of that side saddle stuff.
Rose: You mean, one leg on each side?

Titanic

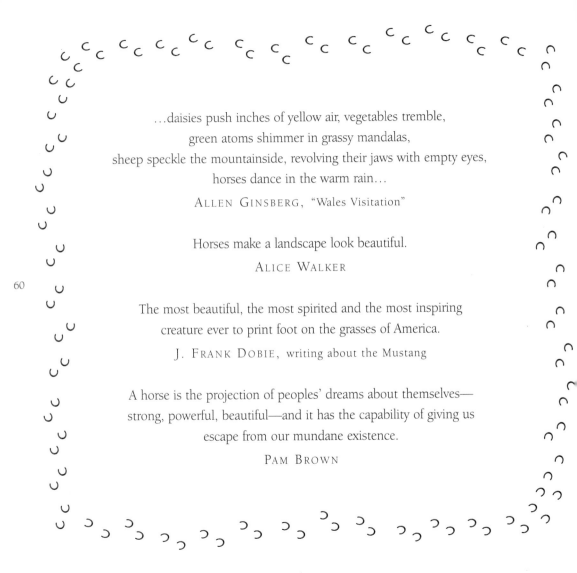

...daisies push inches of yellow air, vegetables tremble,
green atoms shimmer in grassy mandalas,
sheep speckle the mountainside, revolving their jaws with empty eyes,
horses dance in the warm rain...

ALLEN GINSBERG, "Wales Visitation"

Horses make a landscape look beautiful.

ALICE WALKER

The most beautiful, the most spirited and the most inspiring
creature ever to print foot on the grasses of America.

J. FRANK DOBIE, writing about the Mustang

A horse is the projection of peoples' dreams about themselves—
strong, powerful, beautiful—and it has the capability of giving us
escape from our mundane existence.

PAM BROWN

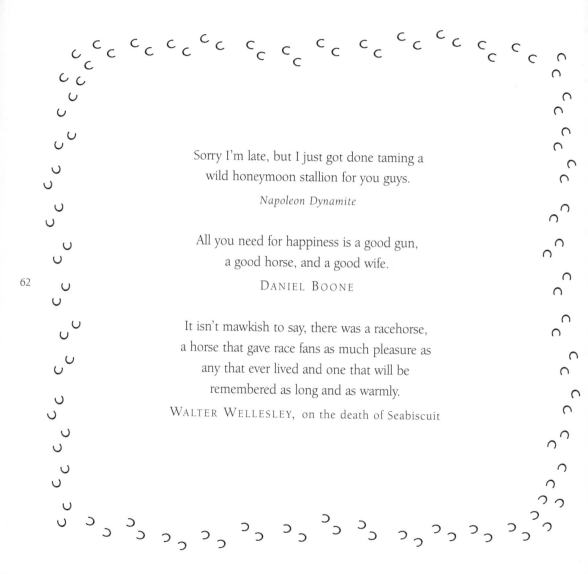

Sorry I'm late, but I just got done taming a
wild honeymoon stallion for you guys.

Napoleon Dynamite

All you need for happiness is a good gun,
a good horse, and a good wife.

DANIEL BOONE

It isn't mawkish to say, there was a racehorse,
a horse that gave race fans as much pleasure as
any that ever lived and one that will be
remembered as long and as warmly.

WALTER WELLESLEY, on the death of Seabiscuit